From the Night Album

From the Night Album

by Jane O. Wayne

Pecan Grove Press San Antonio, Texas

Cover painting by Sheldon S. Helfman
Cover design by Judy S. Thompson

ISBN: 1-931247-38-2

Pecan Grove Press
Box AL
1 Camino Santa Maria
San Antonio, TX 78228

Acknowledgments

Grateful acknowledgment is made to the editors of the publications in which these poems first appeared:

The American Scholar: "When It Lifts"

Boulevard: "Matinee," "Burnt Toast" and "In a Bed North of Sleep"

Chariton Review: "Subterranean," "Omen at Alsancak," "Aftermath," "The Girl from Howth" and "Jeweled Sequence"

Delmar: "From the Night Album"

The Journal: "Romance"

Journal of the American Medical Association: "A Quick Lesson"

Midwest Quarterly: "The Answer After a Pause"

Natural Bridge: "In an Old Desk," "Night Travel" and "Blind Spots"

New Harvest Anthology: "Timed Exposure"

Sagarin Review: "In a Closed Car" and "Long Distance"

The Seattle Review: "The Neglected"

Sou'wester: "The True Freezing Point," "Splendor," "Near Bellecombe," "*Acqua Alta*" and "In a Furnished Flat"

River Styx: "Fundamental Forces" and "Souvenirs"

wordvirtual.com: "Bookmarks."

"Endangered Species" first appeared in the anthology *Poems to Make us Smile* (London, MQ Publications); "On a Clothesline between Two Pines," in *Poems to Calm the Soul* (London, MQP) and "Girl Writing," in the anthology *Heart to Heart* (Abrams), 2001.

I wish to thank my friends Allison Funk and Jason Sommer for their careful readings, suggestions, and encouragement.

For my husband, Shelly

Contents

From the Night Album / 11
Summertime / 12
Near Bellecombe / 13
On the Staircase / 15
The Omen at Alsancak / 16
Blind Spots / 17
In a Closed Car / 18
True Freezing Point / 19
In an Old Desk / 21
Your Familiar / 22
The Narrowing World / 23
On Wide-Lined Paper / 24
Girl Writing / 25
Matinee / 26
The Girl from Howth / 27
Timed Exposure / 28
Getting Results / 30
Subterranean / 31
On a Clothesline between Two Pines / 32
Endangered Species / 33
The Fundamental Forces / 34
The Small Returns / 35
Splendor / 36
Leaps / 37
Jewelled Sequence / 38
Aftermath / 39
Souvenirs / 41

Bookmarks / 42
Soon Enough / 43
At La Garenne / 44
A Quick Lesson / 46
Long Distance / 47
Room-in-Progress / 48
The Collection / 49
The Neglected / 50
Another Winter / 51
Visits / 52
Romance / 53
In a Different Light / 54
In a Bed North of Sleep / 55
The Division / 56
In Our Neighborhood / 57
Burnt Toast / 58
Acqua Alta / 59
In a Furnished Flat / 61
Attrition / 64
Through the Blue Door / 65
The Second Time / 67
At the Flute and Santoor *Jugalbandhi* / 68
Interstices / 69
Night Travel / 70
The Answer after a Pause / 71
When It Lifts / 72
Passage / 73

From the Night Album

A woman steps out of a family album,
and room by room, she walks
through a large house turning off the lights.

When the last light dims, she climbs out of a window
and regards the house from her own death.
Of course, it's only a dream—so the scene can change

to a desk where a man who knows her secrets
is putting them in order. Here, there are no walls
to keep the woman from drifting to a beach.

Here, too, she can watch both the man in the room
and the tide obsessing over the sand
as if the next wave could get it right.

And he goes on—the man at the desk—
arranging a child's set of blocks
inscribed with cryptograms.

Now only a hand appears on a book,
and though she isn't visible, she knows she's older.
Then the pages start flipping

back to front, and she is racing to keep up:
her heart gets faster, the pages smaller.
In all of this, no one says a word.

Summertime

Back then—the old house
still new to us—on long afternoons of work
when even in a shade-drawn room

veils of heat shimmered off the walls,
he might put down a paint brush to go outside,
and from the front porch I'd watch him

set out on his bike. Along the park
where the street slopes, he would start to glide
like a man absolved of gravity—

feet resting on the pedals, arms loose
at his side, while sinking into the wicker chair
some other force relaxed in me.

I could sense the balancing of ease
and effort, that momentary truce like the shade itself
hovering—until the tires, too, turned lazy

and in one smooth motion he'd lean forward
on the handlebars and resume pedaling.
Then I'd just watch—his back,

his damp-streaked shirt pulled taut
across the shoulder blades, that solitary figure
growing smaller in the distance—

as if I knew at the time that I was practicing,
keeping him in sight till where the houses stop
the road sweeps slowly to the left.

Near Bellecombe

Nothing of interest—we were told
before we set out in the heat,
and still as if we expected more

after browsing those few streets,
we circled the aisles
of the church and cemetery.

Then was it the houses
shuttered for the afternoon,
the red geraniums left out in pots,

or the door closed on the only restaurant
that made us stop
outside the dirty windows of that storefront?

To peer in, we had to climb onto a stone ledge
and press our faces to the glass.
When we gripped the wooden panels,

the weathered paint was rough as bark.
Boards gone back to trees, I thought.
Were we too late?

Inside, the gloom held shelves
where we could make out bolts of fabric in a jumble
like crayons stuffed into a half-empty box,

and near the wall a sewing machine without a lid,
its metal torso draped in cobwebs.
Chairs, tables, floors—everything was cloaked in dust,

so much left behind, but nothing to take away,
no clues, no answers,
unless one could count that chair—

the kind we sit on in the house we're visiting—
a slight ladder-back with rush-woven seat
toppled over near the wall.

Hands cupped around my eyes,
I tried to picture it, blinkered out the day
to bring the darkness into focus.

Did they leave slowly,
some movement toward the door
you'd hardly notice—the progress

of a needle along a seam, or was it abrupt—
one of those spools leaping from a lap, its thread
unwound along the floor?

On the Staircase

After the long day's dash-and-spin
comes the slow-down
when a woman follows
a man up a wooden staircase,
the outlines of a suit, a long fitted-dress
climbing steadily, until the curve
of the low ceiling forces them
to bend their heads, then at the landing
where the stairs turn and the walls narrow
to exclude us, the scene abruptly shifts:
an empty park, the kind with gravel paths,
trees in rows, wrought iron benches
from another century.

Did I mention it's all in black and white?
How where the walls start to tunnel
up the stairs and we lose sight of them,
words catch in our throats?
Or that downstairs in the entryway
hung upside down to dry
the ribbed black wings
of an umbrella sleep quietly?
Oh, I'm telling it out of order,
but this is how it happens
on the stairs when we're unable
to call out, to stop them
in the film about us.

The Omen at Alsancak

Tourists that day—
the two of us boarded the ferry
to cross the bay to Karşiyaka
as if we could flee the heat,
the sun-drenched pier
where three local women,
black-garbed head to toe,
waited years ago
for the boat to Konak.

Their August silence
must have warned me
all the way home—
three black birds now
pecking at November,
getting nothing
from the empty street
outside a mourner's house.

Blind Spots

First it was Vermeer—the lemon-yellow
of the woman's dress against
the apron's vibrant blue

and on everything in the scullery
the painted light I'd almost missed—
then the conversation turned

to vision, how you had to train
your eyes on your desk
to see a certain glow between

the study window and the carpet,
and I thought of mirrors—
some self there that's fugitive,

not the eye-to-eye, but the sidelong,
the off-guard a camera catches.
And that other childhood game

played against our boredom—
long summer afternoons when we'd repeat
a word to empty it of meaning:

word, word, word spun out
till we grew light-headed,
the same dizziness

close to one another now—your face
dissolving into separate features,
the walls gone flimsy,

then a few steps back to let the painting
reassemble where it hangs—stranger
back to lover.

In a Closed Car

As a child it always came over me
in the closed car on the way to visit
my father's mother at the nursing home:
that sudden sinking
in a bag of kittens, and the rock
weighing me down—motion itself
pulling me under.
The whole ride there
against that forced embrace—fumes
of gasoline, of cigarettes, of dread
rising in my nostrils, nausea
bulging in my throat—I closed my eyes.
When I opened the tight collar
of my Sunday coat, some other passenger
sighed in me. That sigh still surfaces
through a haze of smoke.
In the back seat with the windows up,
I can hear a hollow tapping
against the metal tray, the same hand
flicking off the ashes, flicking
petals from a rose.
When the sun glares at a certain angle,
I can't see where I'm going.

True Freezing Point

1

No one warned her
that if she stayed while it settled in,
she would breathe its whiteness in the room,
would feel its hand on her shoulder,
metal-cold, sticking to the skin,
and in her bones
would take on sudden knowledge
as of a point attained, some furthest reach,
say a tide, a solstice
or the kind of limit that a climber meets
before the doubling-back begins.
Then so quiet next to him,
she can hear the landscape change,
flesh becoming fossil
in a bed of stone.
Wherever she turns now
the compass needle in her faces north.
November, numbness
filling her gloves from the fingers up—
this is the true freezing point,
the glacier no one can live on.

2

Is this what's left—this wood pile
more like sticks than logs
to get her through the winter?
She has heard the thunder of the ax,
the moment when the log splits
dividing the years into before and after.
Now she starts walking away,
counting the days, dragging a long shadow,
like luggage, up a hill.
The violin-maker told her

that you have to coax the wood
into being a violin, that it always wants
to go back to being a tree. Each fiber in her
understands. Women, violins—
if no one holds them in the dead of winter
they go back to wood.

3

Some nights, with the lights out
she gets up to prowl
like a trespasser in her own house.
White-gowned, she drifts
across the living room—a full moon
across a dark sky—then moving on,
room by room, the way a hand
might search a chest of drawers,
she roams the whole house,
her bare feet reclaiming it.
Not even a handkerchief across a face
could move so carefully—upstairs, down,
then up again—her body and her mind
some liquid medium a sculptor pours
to fill an empty mold.

In an Old Desk

Open the top drawer of this desk
and you're on the threshold of a musty house.
A lone pencil rolls along the corridor,
and nothing buffers it.
Then the bottom drawer drags
like a trunk lugged across a wooden floor.
Inside, a few faded snapshots
have despaired of finding albums.
They're either creased, or curling at the edges,
and leaf-brittle to the touch.
Right under them
where a rubber-band crumbled
some letters drift out
like sheep through a hole in a fence,
but no one rounds them up:
a flock of envelopes with canceled stamps,
faded ink on faded stationery.
Here when I pry off a paper-clip
embedded in a page,
it leaves a rusty kiss.
You've been gone long enough
for glue to harden in the bottle.
Nothing stays the same
except the climate in the closed drawer:
always overcast and snowing
dust on love-letters.

Your Familiar

On a warm night
when there's no one else around,
lifting a shirt over your head
you might have pulled a bottle-stopper
to release some essence—a spectral self
between the cloth and skin
that drifts as you undress—
its weightlessness no more than billows
in the bedroom curtains.
As you lie down, you picture mist
rising from a field, the field's contour
echoed in the haze. So vigilant by then,
you could have heard a sigh
escaping near your pillow—air
joining air, the last hint of it
dispersing in the dark,
like a spirit from a body.

The Narrowing World

It starts.
Not the whole room,
just the flowered wall-paper
beside the crib
where instead of napping
when the shades were drawn,
you would watch
a wedge of light drag across the wall.
Then another scene:
the same wall where you stood
at the mahogany dresser
while she brushed your hair.
Young, three at most
and there in the frame, the same distance
from the glass as you—that stranger
who lowered her brow
when you did. Point
and she'd point back, anticipate
your every gesture, eye to eye.
The outward. The inward.
And in that meeting, no allure
or aversion—just a face,
fait accompli, the recognition
that wherever you went
you'd be coupled with it,
not be whom you expected
at your own door.
Nothing was said,
but didn't queasiness
fill the space between you?

On Wide-Lined Paper

Again the drowsy clouds
through sky-high windows,
and the room that boxed us in,

the banner of alphabet
wrapped around its walls,
desks lined up

like numbers in a column,
and the fresh sheet of paper
that started the day:

name and date top-right,
hand tensed around a yellow pencil,
then in drawn-out silences

between each spelling word
the first answers
that spilled onto the page,

pell-mell as a toss of jacks,
were followed by a panic
of erasers, a vacillation

that rubbed the letters
into streak and scratch,
until the guesses we handed in

were ghost-layered palimpsests—
all our faults etched
in the soft paper's stone memory.

Girl Writing

from Milton Avery's painting

If you didn't stop in front of her,
you might only glimpse the target-red of socks,
and legs white as ropes, twined around each other.

You'd have to pause before you'd see
a girl staring at a desk, face flushed and eye-less,
her left-handed pen already at the bottom of the page.

From a foot away it looks easy—all of it—
just patches of pure color.
You'd think he took them straight out of their tubes

as we did crayons from a box—
paint smoothed on
the way a knife spreads mustard over bread.

Step back again and yes—the face is featureless,
the feet larger than the head, and one arm
bluer than the other.

Portrait maybe—since someone says his daughter
posed for it—but nothing one can quarrel with,
not a likeness to hold to the original.

Still how much life hides behind the lies the painter tells:
the too-pink face, the floating desk,
the letter that's never mailed.

Here in a quiet room that has no door to close,
the furniture won't wear out. No one will buy the table,
no one inherit the wooden bench and move away.

Matinee

Bring me back her lung and liver as a token.
Brothers Grimm

In the forest of that movie theater
where I peeked out, not through trees but fingers,
and my legs dangled from the leather seat,

even if my feet didn't touch the ground
where Snow White scurried—I held my breath
between the lightning and the thunder.

And when the queen snarled in the castle,
green and yellow flesh dripping down her cheeks
like candle-wax I was mesmerized, backed into my chair

until that taloned finger pointed at the magic glass;
then jumping to the ground, I turned,
stumbled past a row of legs like tree stumps.

Such cackling at my back—the whole time
I was breathless—the aisle itself oppressive as a hill
and how far the door,

the small red embers of the exit sign.
I knew before I got outside
the slap of daylight wouldn't bring me to.

Wherever I'd go there'd be no mirror
safe from her, no kingdom that she didn't rule.
Over the din of traffic—cars, pedestrians—

I could hear a croaking
in the distance—some black bird
that can tear the flesh from bone.

The Girl from Howth

for Maeve

Not Daphne
running from Apollo in the woods—
but daughter, flesh-and-bone girl,
a blue-jeaned innocent
fleeing something
no one else could see,
something hounding her
all the way through childhood.
It must have followed her
home from school
or in the field that afternoon
must have trampled the knee-high grass
until she reached the cliff
where rocks shift underfoot.
On a clear day like this,
the sunlit sea is dazzling,
making it hard for us to know
what monster-melancholy
must have pounded at her like the sea,
what stone-grinding argument
a girl alone could lose out here.
She must have heard
something we can't hear—
some thunder in her
louder than the waves
working boulders into sand.

Timed Exposure

We don't know the place or country
in this blurred photograph
my grandmother left in a box of documents,

or the white-bearded relative,
who stands tall before a sunlit column,
the man himself a column, feet together,

hands pocketed in the open overcoat he wears
above another full-length coat,
or why just then he stopped

whatever he was doing
to have his picture taken in his hat—
eyes narrowed for the sun, brows lowered

in what seems a frown till at closer look
the way he holds our gaze
shows something mild, something easy in a man

who wears a tie knotted at the throat,
but whose half-buttoned vest
droops open in the middle,

whose too-long-sleeves are stacked
with creases wrist-to-elbow.
His shoes are worn, some tired second skin

that barely hides its bones.
He could be tired, too. And there's a hint,
I think, of gentleness around his mouth

which might have widened to a smile
or words perhaps—some levity
beyond the camera's reach.

Before? After?
Conjecture, of course, when what survives
is only this enlarged photograph

reducing him to moments.
Think, then, of stopping on that street,
a letter not yet posted

or travel papers to fill out,
and standing by that wall—
the cold of idleness, of interruption,

the open lens and how long it must have seemed
before some other hand
capped off a certain measurement of light.

Getting Results

Early March and the sun's come out,
the air's soft again,

but in the winter of this office
where I wait for answers

the only thing I'll later recall
the white table holds

is a jar of cotton clouds.
The floor, the walls—

everything's white
except a gray curtain of film

a woman holds to a back-lit glass
as if she's merely testing

china to the light. I should have
heeded my own footsteps

in the hall, the hollow echo
in my wake, should have

seen it coming: bones
less porcelain than lace—

a hip, a spine, a wrist,
a paper snowflake in a window.

Subterranean

If you go down there alone,
the bogeyman will get you.

Mondays—for detergent smells and bleach,
and the washer's rhythmic thud,
blades agitating sheets and towels,
and from its open tub, slow rising suds
as shivery as milk-bubbles that we blew
through straws—we would venture
halfway down the stairs.

It wasn't words we heeded
but the rough-stone walls—corners full
of spider webs—and the concrete floor
where whatever tripped the spring
left nothing in the wooden trap but the gore
of our imaginings. Every basement since
has been that one—the year-round snow

of plaster-dust, the damp, the gray,
the pipe's sporadic flush, then that gargling
in the throaty sewer, its grate-like eyes
fixed on us, and nothing to fend off darkness
but a naked light-bulb dangling from a cord
and what scurried into crevices
when the light came on still waiting.

On a Clothesline between Two Pines

Summer and the cool of early morning,
a faded version of the moon
still in the sky,
then just the driftwood-gray clothespins
and the white of the towel
forgotten on the line,
the night's damp still in it,
and not much else
except that somehow we'd crossed over,
opened our eyes
or splashed our faces at the sink,
that there were stones to touch
and thoughts we couldn't,
and now unfolding chairs:
canvas snapping into place,
wooden legs settling
into sand under us,
that all of this could happen,
that it could stop,
not just dreams, but sleep itself,
rain, mist, evaporation.

Endangered Species

The resins used to make products permanently
wrinkle-resistant invade the very structure of the cotton.
from an advertisement

No crumpling from a drawer then,
or creases from a crowded closet,
not even a hanger's shoulder marks,

and picture meeting on the street
a worn summer suit or dress
like a blank expression on a face:

none of those sit-stripes on our laps,
or pleats up and down our sleeves
flexing like an accordion.

And what about the nervous tucks
a hand leaves in a handkerchief
or the long day's corrugations in our socks?

Just look—the way your shirt sprawls now
on the bedroom floor, loose folds
like a lowered sail,

and the denim pool you're wading,
one foot, then the other stepping
from its ripples.

Think of the loss. No matter what we did,
our sheets and pillowcases
smooth as ice—after as before.

The Fundamental Forces

Astonishing—the tug—
not just dust to corners, or moon-driven tides
but the sway on everything,
the push-and-pull that one can't argue with.
A gate sags. A can of paint explodes.
So much occurs in spite of us.
Even in the shower,
the water whirling down the drain
pulls at us: its suction on the foot,
like an oppressive kiss.
And doesn't yearning itself demonstrate
the law of gravity—the constant pull
of one body on another?
We meet. We cross a room, moved
like iron filings in a magnetic field.
The curtain billows in the dark. A loose spring
rattles in the bed. The force
that holds together particles
holds us.

The Small Returns

You used to smile
at how lightly our Japanese house guest
entered a room
and pulled a door into its frame
without a sound
as if the plaster walls and the wood
were shoji screens.
How much we learn from entrances:
my rush-and-slams,
our daughters' detonations,
and what about your signature—
a certain trudge, a solidness,
some low note played on a cello?
I never told you
how day after day the back steps' groan
or the whine and shudder of the screen-door
could take my breath away.
A knob, a latch, the thinnest metal click—
and I'd stop like a hunted animal
listening for a twig to break
till you called out
and something in the woods retreated.

Splendor

Let him have you,
but first let him come in all his glory.
Metamorphoses, Ovid

Out of the cold soil,
this single tulip in my garden raises its head—
its red almost painful next to green.
And what if my dead came back,
visited, like a god—
some charged current traveling the air
and, head to toe, the same lightning
that can slash a tree wide open,
flashing down my side?
Out here on the lawn,
wouldn't his softest word
thunder in my ear,
and what about his touch—
wouldn't I perish under its white heat
as Semele did when she met
what she was longing for?

Leaps

The day after he died
there was a moment
when the phone rang
and half-asleep
in your reading chair
you waited for him
to answer it upstairs.
The lamp on, the book
face-down on your lap,
you must have drifted,
stopped along that wooden bridge
to watch a swarm of carp
ruffling the water,
then out of the pond
before the eye could reel it in,
a splash, a breathless glistening—
in the room itself
each dazzling moment
a kind of arc inscribed in air.

Jewelled Sequence

That evening on my bike
when I took the wrong road
I could hear the splash-and-shuffle
of the swamp, the alligator-mud
waking up. I tried to get home,
but a spider web snared me—
the more I pulled the worse the tangles,
sticky threads like spun-sugar
on my face and fingers.
Turning pages then,
I was looking through a scrapbook
full of treasures, jewels like flowers
pressed between the pages.
I knew at the time it couldn't be,
but somehow this took place
inside our living room—
the change of scene as effortless
as slides projected on a wall.
Hand to hand, a group of us
seated in a circle passed the book
like a platter at a table. By morning
when it came back to me
it was empty. Does it matter less
that this never happened,
or that after the rain I can see the world
turned over in a puddle—
only darker?

Aftermath

Turn on the light in here
and it gets dimmer—the kind of pall
one light-bulb less in a fixture casts on everything.

Even furnished, the house gives off
the white hush of a seashell, the spirit-echo
heard in naked rooms.

Things are wood that weren't:
the spot where he stood, his words.
How solid absence is

and palpable—
the furrow in the mattress next to me
that won't smooth out.

Some days the kettle boils
until nothing is left.
I turn my back on everything.

In the sink, fat whitens in a black skillet.
A week of dishes wait: mustard, catsup, eggs—
like paints hardening on a palette.

Outside the kitchen window
the scarecrow waits for the wind,
his old shirt and jeans

motionless among the vacant vines.
Foolish—holding on
the way a mirror holds a glance—

I should wear white
and leave the windows wide open in the house.
I should turn the mirrors to the wall

and study every detail of the green world,
like some letter that before tearing up
one might memorize.

Souvenirs

From that long summer on the coast—
only a seashell on our mantle, and his two smiles
in black and white, a part for the whole.

And it's a weeknight then, just an ordinary dinner
at the kitchen table where he sits:
his plate half-filled, his fork stopped in air,

and a static smile that pretends to nothing else
before or after. But see in the other one
how he refutes himself—only moments later—

the narrowed eyes, the mouth twisted
in the strangest part of the laugh
that flashed across his face (more cry perhaps

than laugh) that seems to say, *everything's in motion*:
each moment a departure, a passenger
waving from a train window, one compartment

then another pulling away, car after car
passing the platform where we stand
outside the photographs.

Bookmarks

Hard bound, soft bound, even magazines you visit
have your calling cards.
You never slam a door behind you.

On these shelves in almost every book you've read,
assorted scraps stick out
like loose threads from a carpet's fringe.

Cardboard leans like tombstones;
softer papers bend like banners
in a wind that no one notices.

Postcards, envelopes,
movie tickets, shopping lists,
you leave anything in reach that's flat enough—

some strings, some ribbons,
and here's a nail file
wedged into a dictionary.

When you turn pages,
moving forward in a book
you must struggle with a counter urge

that slows you down, some stealthy child
who's trailing bread crumbs.
Each flap of paper leads you back:

a passage underlined, a circled word or phrase, a chapter
like an island-paradise you left
hoping to return.

Soon Enough

Sometimes when a key
turns in an ignition
there's a brief grinding
that gets your hopes up
before the battery goes dead.
If he listens carefully
he can hear it as he's waking up
or as he carries luggage
down the stairs
to leave the house.
For days he'll plod along
digging his heels into a horse
that won't move faster.
But soon enough
he'll come to a place in the field
where the footpath disappears
and a load he can't put down
gets heavier.
Somehow in the time allotted
he'll get across; he'll find a city
and keep walking
till he reaches a busy intersection
where an old man runs after a bus
as it leaves the curb
and a boy watches from the sidewalk.

At La Garenne

A bird's unfamiliar song, the floorboards
creaking underfoot in a foreign language—
nothing is certain in the dusk.

Here when she lies down
under the mosquito net, she can't tell
east from west. The walls sag

and slowly out of the thick mist
in the far corner of the field
a white horse takes shape.

All around her, there's the pull
of something that has no face, no name
to weigh it down, only figments—

a shadow bird that sweeps across the path,
a lizard scurrying into a crevice
between sleeping and waking.

Last night her own cry pulled her out of her sleep
as from a burning house, a dream
she can't bring herself to repeat in the morning.

Instead she'll tell you the part
about the footsteps crunching over gravel
that she heard from bed,

or how running to the window she could see
in the first light, a man arriving from the garden,
the head in his hand turning into lettuce.

She knows when she leaves the room,
the cold mirror will hold her face
as it would a breath.

It's not easy after sleeping in another idiom
to descend the narrow stairs,
luggage in both hands,

or to turn an oval knob without waking
the three dogs that sleep behind the kitchen door
of a half-remembered fairy tale.

A Quick Lesson

You might have left it out overnight,
the way it's lying in the shade near your swing,
its brindled fur smooth as a new toy animal's.

It lets you hunker down to get a closer look,
even lets you nudge it in the side—the same prod
you'd use to wake the cat

though this sleeper doesn't startle
toward the privet-hedge. Nothing happens
until you claim it with both hands,

then what was docile on the ground
takes on a cardboard-stiffness—
some stronger hold than yours already on it.

There's a moment—still cradling it—
when whatever stopped in the garden
makes you stop—and in the hush

though you're far too young
to ask if it weighs now what it did before,
if the life in it weighed nothing

you must be weighing
something in your mind
before you let it go: rabbit and all.

Long Distance

Not yet dawn
when the phone shrills
through my sleep
like an alarm clock,
and behind your hurried voice
is the echo of the call-box,
a din of cars, pedestrians,
then a coin tumbling, like a pinball
through the conversation—
more hurried talk punctuated
by more coins jangling.

You could be downstairs
late for school again, one arm
in a jacket, the other full of books,
instead of standing on a street,
a different climate,
different time zone, while here
wandering absently,
I find myself, when the coins
and words run out, sitting on your bed,
the receiver like an empty conch
purling at my ear.

Room-in-Progress

There's a kind of trespass in a cemetery
that occurs in empty rooms:
the sanded floors, the white
of freshly painted walls,
no mirrors, no photographs,
nothing hanging on the walls or windows,
and even without a bed
one can sense a sleeper lingering,
some prior claim,
like a spirit tending its bones.
If you doubt it, just stand here
alone on a winter day.

The slightest movement
makes the room echo, some call
whose words one can't make out—
a summons maybe, or a muffled threat.
I know how it goes. Bring in a chair, a desk
or even lamp—and everything will change.
Can't you feel the pressure
building up around the vacant room,
all the trappings of domestic life
getting ready? Each time I leave,
I close the door—finger-in-dike
against the rising tide of furniture.

The Collection

Without looking we used to find them
with missing rungs or legs,
cane or wicker seats caved in,
or a rocker without rockers.
People would discard them near a curb
or in a back alley where we'd happen on them
like foundlings on church steps.
We couldn't pass them by. We had a call,
a missionary's zeal for derelicts.
We brought each castoff home—
instinct driving us, like crows
with nesting matter in their beaks.

Once mended, they'd find a niche
to suit them—at a dressing table, say,
or a desk looking out a window.
A few settled down near the fireplace;
others wedged in like late arrivals at a party,
knee-to-knee beneath the crowded table.
In time, each staked out its territory,
took over corners, blocked halls
and entryways. While some held boxes
on their laps, others waited vacantly
to stub our toes or bang us in the shins
unless we stepped aside.

The Neglected

Just now I stumbled upon that room
where she was sitting on the same sofa—
not dead after all.

But something had changed. Was it the drawn
shades that spoke of reluctance, the light
the green of algae in a fish bowl?

I couldn't catch her eyes, her face
the blur that takes flight from a branch
before binoculars can steady,

and the whole time only a hint of words—
her wavery voice moving in and out of range
like music on a radio.

Then a sudden sinking
where I stood (a soft carpet maybe),
losing ground in any case—

no argument, no arm strong enough
to bring her back across the border
of awakening. So loss again.

This time mixed with knowing
I'd visited before and come home
empty-handed, that what emerges in the dark—

the tired woman on the tired sofa,
the tired room itself—has been there all along:
not just friend, neighbor, intimate,

but all my dead relegated to some attic
of the mind, all my ghosts
waiting on hangers to be worn.

Another Winter

The first cold day
when I took out my brown tweed coat—
its bulk, its leathery buttons,
the lining, slippery and cold—
I didn't know I was putting on
an old November.
The dead are always near,
so matter of fact
you might not notice them,
but we don't have to tiptoe
through their rooms
or turn the doorknob carefully
as if a child's asleep.
They dance the slow blur
in photographs, and we can hear them
in the brittle leaves,
teaching us dust.

Visits

In a burst
as when you lift a lid from boiling water
he comes back:
a penciled note tucked inside a book,
or a jar of salvaged varnish
crusted over, like a scab.
The house is mined.
A plate breaks; a kitchen chair
teeters on hind legs; even bread-crumbs
careless on a stick of butter can explode.
You've happened onto gloves
buried under papers,
or on the bottom of a drawer
a roll of film that's been exposed.
That's all it takes.
A room can give off sparks
the way a burning log does—
bright visits that you're never ready for.
When you tear a rag in two
it's not shredding you hear
but a dust-cloth reverting to a shirt.

Romance

Not so much behind us then,
so still unspoiled
and eager to repeat
the passages we loved,
to watch your hand lift
the record player's arm in air
and move it back in time
to the perimeter—
the smoothest part
where silence whirls
black and satiny
before the music starts,
and starts to dull.
Then not too long
before the ashtray fills,
the quiet settles in,
and in the matchbook
where the matches used to stand
like trees in serried ranks,
you leave the front cover
tucked behind the stumps
to show you're through.

In a Different Light

How slowly we approached that hill
in the distance that is no longer a hill,
no longer another land.

Late in the day whatever we touch
is doubled here. Shadow-selves
stretch out behind us on the ground.

I keep pulling the same dandelion
out of different lawns, cutting
the same red rose for the table.

Everything is something else in addition
to itself: the black dog barking at the door
is a white dog barking at another.

In this crowded house an old mirror
multiplies the rooms—rooms full of other rooms,
other chairs, other faces.

I didn't know that a single dove could call
from so many trees at once,
or one doorknob open so many doors.

We're never alone. Even outside
when I bent down to tie my shoelace
under a pink-flowering tree

I found those saffron petals
strewn on a white stone floor again,
dust-coated feet walking on them.

In a Bed North of Sleep

. . . the feeling that they have dug a hundred holes
in the walls of the house and lurk inside them.
Letter to Max Brod, Dec. 1917
Franz Kafka

On long nights in a narrow bed
pulling up the blanket, he listens to wind wheeze
through the house's cracks and joints.

A branch rubs against the roof's gutter—
bone against bone, the winter's jaws
gnashing on nothing.

Then so quiet in the room
he can hear dust fall out of the air,
can hear words whisper in a closed book.

Will it ever end—the cough, the cover slipping
from his neck, the crust of bread he left
curling slowly on its plate?

There's no sanctuary.
Even the plaster walls are thin as flesh
where some nocturnal nerve flares up.

Once the scratching starts,
he's wide awake—the glacial floor impassable,
the door across the room remote as morning.

The rest is intervals:
fits of rustling, fits of silence.
All sorts of mice oppress him in the dark.

The Division

What catches the eye
is not the heavy coat on a mild day,

but how the bearded man across the street
puts his face so close to the wall, he could be kissing it.

The sun's just right so he moves himself,
the way you'd turn a lens to bring an image into focus,

back and forth until the shadow
on the wall is sharp enough.

Once in place, he barely stirs except to shuffle
side-to-side, his partner blindly following.

Horns honk, pedestrians walk by, but he's in private,
absorbed as any man shaving at a mirror,

a kind of street narcissus trapped in that dark pool,
until a struggle slowly starts, a restlessness

that's in the twist of neck and shoulders,
the arm's slight sway. And even if we can't hear

from where we sit in the restaurant, we can tell
by the way he shakes his head and waves his fists

he's on the losing end, till in one of those lulls
when the sidewalk's empty, he backs away

so there's room to hurl an arm pointblank—
its pistol-finger pointed at the target.

In Our Neighborhood

For all we know, she's inside
humming to herself,
some radio tuned to a station that's off the air.

Who would notice
if without moving she leaves the table,
leaves the room behind as a cicada does a shell,

everything in place,
not even a chair pulled out from the table?
Maybe now she's in the hall upstairs

opening doors to rooms she's never seen—
a stranger in her own house.
She'd have nothing to lose,

her pockets already inside-out
like burst pods of milkweed dangling from a bush.
While we pause under the streetlight,

she could be lost in a forest of furniture,
ready to step outside the halo
her flashlight casts on the ground.

Burnt Toast

If you eat the charred part, it keeps the wolf away.
Armenian folk advice

Another morning, another newspaper on the lawn,
and all the way to the park,
the dog pulling the leash,
the pebble in her shoe getting larger.
So cold the yews blacken. If she's not careful,
she could close one eye to winter
and flatten it all. She could be the tethered creature
that paws a circle in the dust.

When she came home, she must have hung up her coat,
must have set the breakfast table.
The refrigerator drones on, background
becoming foreground: or is it the snow
falling on snow—so white it threatens to erase itself—
that holds her in its spell?
The knife spreads butter over the toast without her,
as if the body moves on without the soul.

Acqua Alta

The evening our boat arrived in the rain,
was it travel fatigue, a certain haziness
that cast a spell over everything,
or the island itself so shrouded in fog
you had to take it on faith?

It was dark by the time
we reached the flat on foot
and in our neighborhood the slots
meant to drain the pavement
were already backing up like sinks.

Later before bed, when sirens
lured us back outside—not for fire,
but water—we were youths again,
breaking rules about night
we didn't know we had.

Everywhere we walked, some ancient god
had come to life, crossing thresholds,
climbing stairways into shops and houses.
We could hear its wrath rising
in canals, in rhythmic slapping

at back windows and barricaded doors.
Closer to the waterfront,
we had to walk on knee-high planks
that bridged the pooling water.
Most of the time we went single file,

umbrellas isolating us until we reached
the main piazza. There where we stopped
to rest under the arcade, though shops
were closed, all around us in the dark
cameras flashed like sparklers.

Without warning then,
it started up on the far shore
of the ephemeral lake—piano music
pouring out through open hotel-doors
to where we stood. I can still hear it if I try,

not the song, it's forgotten, but the sound
the piano made: the music amplified
by all the stone and darkness,
and the water echoing—a rowboat-voice
calling all the way from childhood.

In a Furnished Flat

Here it takes a few days to learn
the front-left burner's trick of going out
when the flame's lowered
and which way the faucets turn,

but nothing disappoints us:
not the dust or the four-flights up,
or the half-step between the dining
and living rooms that we keep stumbling on.

Even after a week when I pick up
the green-enameled pot
I get the slightest jolt of the unfamiliar
from its handle.

His family has rented to us as is
so where we sleep the bedside table
holds a stack of readings
in philosophy, some poetry in French,

a German novel, bookmark still in place—
everything in this Pompeii of rooms
the way he left it: the clock plugged in,
the drawers and closets full,

and on his desk the usual disarray—pens,
papers, books—along with family photographs.
One turn-of-the-century couple poses
in front of *trompe l'oeil* flowers and columns,

another post-war bride and groom
in a living room, then on a country road
the same couple, middle-aged.
In front of them, in a curled snapshot

wedged between the glass and frame,
two boys in shorts are squinting
at the camera, the smaller one caught
fidgeting, one leg coiled around the other.

They're all in black and white,
but nothing recent, no face to put on the man
whom often I picture ahead of me
on the hall stairs. He's in his 40's,

coming home to the dark flat,
briefcase in one hand, umbrella in the other,
the fatigue of that last illness
showing in his gait.

* * *

A whole month sitting in his chairs,
eating from his dishes, even lying on his bed,
and still, like the mixing bowl I dropped,
the shards don't make a whole.

In my mind he was always shorter
than average, a slight man, until
I tried the wrong closet for a broom
where a row of suits and full-length coats

confronted me—their broad shoulders
at eye level. Quickly as if I'd opened
someone's diary, I closed the door.
I never mention to you

how I can be in a café or vaporetto
or just crossing a piazza in the late afternoon,
when out of the crowd,
the way we'd choose an unborn's name,

I choose a face for him.
That first night the city sirens
warned of *acqua alta*,
what else did we assume when we put on

borrowed boots to trudge in the rain
through unknown streets?
It's February—outside and in—
and through these small rooms made smaller

with their walls of books and music,
their photographs and paintings,
we move tentatively across the bare floors,
especially at night in the long corridor

between the bedroom and the bath
where we're reduced to silhouette.
Passing the marble bust, the wood-carved mask,
we grow more bodiless, more ghost

than he—the rightful occupant—
who, while we clink glasses
at the dinner table, hovers just outside
the wavering reaches of the candlelight.

Attrition

The leather-red spine and edges
have worn down to cardboard,

and inside, the fingered tabs have curled up
until the "z" is scarcely legible.

Most of the names have lost their faces
or else their features blur

as when a painter moves a portrait
toward abstraction.

Even their addresses stand like signs
in front of vacant lots.

In what sea, then, has this shell
been scoured—this hand-sized book,

whose scrawl I almost don't recognize
as mine? And you, the one I'm looking for—

what if you've moved,
left no forwarding address?

Through the Blue Door

Near the entry gate to the old quarter
a man offered to show you the way
if you met him here before the sun went down.

Closed doors and shuttered windows,
women in veils: everywhere you looked
the city hid its face, so now quickly in and out

of narrow passageways, you follow the guide
along unpaved streets in the silence of a film
that has no music, no background noise

only the thud of shoes so close
the rhythm seems internal, say of lungs panting,
especially when after too many turns

to find the way back yourself,
he rounds a corner ahead of you,
and for whole moments you lose sight of him.

Past the market place—further into the labyrinth
than you'd risk alone—he leads you
till you come to a blue door without a sign

where knocking once, he steps aside.
Alone there in the frame of the entryway,
as if a shutter clicked, you look out

from a black-and-white photograph you took years ago,
moments only—then in color again and moving
through the open door, slowly steam envelops you

because earlier in the night I had opened a drawer
full of maps that were thin along the creases
from folding and refolding.

Streets were circled, routes penciled in—but above all
it was the hurried scrawl in the margins,
a few addresses and directions that helped me picture

how you might have taken notes
standing at a station or a crowded marketplace.
Some nights you can appear in a lone rowboat

in the middle of a moonlit lake, or I might walk you
to a bridge that reaches further than the eye
or to the mouth of a volcano I've only read about,

but on those used maps the routes were already marked
like questionnaires with blanks filled in—
nothing left to guess, nothing undecided.

The Second Time

The same cobblestones and narrow streets,
step-gabled houses lining canals, boats and drawbridges,
even banners flapping from the balconies—

and where was I? The whole week
standing on some bridge in the mind—*not this, not that*,
but the one from years ago:

dark-brick houses rising
from the water, a mass of willow branches
leafless on the bank—nothing really, but enough now

to overshadow the cyclist brushing my sleeve,
a drawn-out teetering on the cobbled path
before the wheels right themselves—then gone.

Yards ahead of me, you're all eagerness
with a camera, choosing windows, doors,
a church façade, then an arch

that leads to where the canal swerves
into a dark basin. When I join you
on the bridge, you gesture

toward the water, saying something
half-lost to a banner thrashing in the wind,
and though I'm trying,

the winter afternoon is closing in,
and I can't catch up: some past perfect-swan
still in the way, its spell so tight

I nearly miss the now-shimmery version
you point out before it breaks into ripples
near the bridge we're standing on.

At the Flute and Santoor *Jugalbandhi*

Jugalbandhi - binding together or bringing together
(from program notes on an Indian concert)

The second shade
of tangerine in the shot-silk
shirt the flautist wears

ripples in the wind
of the slightest move he makes—
that under-color

fluttering as he plays,
like a billow through a curtain,
the whole time the cloth

on fire with highlights,
the music, too, a shimmering,
the off-and-on

of one of those stars
a crystal flashes on a wall
that's gone before

one points to it—
and next to me your glance,
an iridescence.

Interstices

Again. Like the need for breath,
it sweeps over them.
Then a kiss—that close.
A full embrace.
And in the space between them
that has their shape—
a certain darkness
where the bodies meet,
not from night, but the shadows
cast on one another.
Arms, legs, a Turk's head knot
of limbs—and still some line
of demarcation comes
between the two of them.
Even flesh on flesh,
it's there: some boundary,
dark, indelible,
some bold brush stroke
keeping them apart,
like lovers drawn in ink
that we step back to watch.

Night Travel

When we couldn't sleep last night
you told me your dream
about packing for a trip,

some destination never specified
but clearly urgent,
the last-minute rummaging

that went on and on,
while your movements dragged
as if through thigh-high water.

You were opening a closet—a wet coat,
a leaking roof—when, dream opening
onto dream, it came back to me

that I'd been sorting through
the same drawers and closets,
while a plane (or was it a train?)

its engine running, like a worry
through a head, was somewhere
on the outskirts of the dream

ready to leave without us.
Lying in the dark, we grew quiet
watching headlights sweep the walls,

the incandescent streaks like meteors
across the bedroom sky.
How quickly, too, you drifted off

without me—as if moments earlier
I hadn't heard my dream
first spoken on your lips.

The Answer after a Pause

A certain piano phrase,
maybe that metallic plunk
that frees the kick-stand on the bike,

or eyes that won't hold still,
say a hummingbird
darting at a red flower years ago,

or the scent of thyme,
and some creature barely seen
before it slips between the rocks,

part water, part wind,
lines shimmering on the bottom of a pool,
and peonies, white ones, heavy-headed in a vase,

even petals falling, twilight, too,
the blur of watercolors, blues, pinks—and you,
yes—especially you.

When It Lifts

At the zenith
of rolling up the window shade
there's a falling into place,
a soft snap
when the winding mechanism
catches hold,
pawl in ratchet,
and the taut pull-string
loosens in your hand
so you can let go,
not just to start the morning,
but to put the last darkness
of the room away—
the night itself
no more than a star map
covering a wall
an hour in science class,
then rolled up somewhere
and forgotten.

Passage

Still in my nightclothes
and easy to drift,
to carry the half-filled cup
into the dark of morning
without spilling it,
so I didn't really choose
between the house and garden
as I moved through the doorway,
nothing in mind
except the wooden thuds
of the back steps underfoot—
that solidness while the night itself
gave way, one moment
becoming the next,
until I could see green
and blue, and the starlings
starting up in the trees, wave
after wave taking flight.
Below them on the lawn
I stopped, but the whole summer
pivoted: leaves flickering
recto-verso on the birch
and out of nowhere, a sense of floating
into the next season—
nothing to choose between,
no threshold when I reach
that place where water
flows from one sea into another.

Recent Books from Pecan Grove Press

Barker, Wendy. *Between Frames.* 2006.
ISBN: 1-931247-35-8 $9

Byers, Cluster R. *Revisions of Visions.* 2005.
ISBN: 1-877603-81-3 $12

Challender, Craig. *Dancing on Water.* 2005.
ISBN: 1-931247-20-x $12

Davis, Glover. *Seperate Lives.* 2007.
ISBN: 1-931247-36-6 $9

Emmons, Jeanne. *Baseball Nights and DDT.* 2005.
ISBN: 1-931247-26-9 $12.50

Essbaum, Jill Alexander. Oh Forbidden. 2005.
ISBN: 1-931247-29-3 $9

Fargnoli, Patricia. *Small Songs of Pain.* 2004.
ISBN: 1-931247-17-x $10

Gutierrez, Cesar. *Lomesome Pine.* 2006.
ISBN: 1-931247-31-5 $9

Haddad, Marian. *Somewhere Between Mexico and a River Called Home.* 2004. ISBN: 1-931247-18-8 $15

Hochman, Will. *Freer.* 2006.
ISBN: 1-931247-34-x $15

Hughes, Glenn. *Sleeping at the Open Window.* 2005.
ISBN: 1-931247-25-0 $8

Hunley, Tom C. *My Life as a Minor Character.* 2005.
ISBN: 1-931247-27-7 $8

Kasper, Catherine. *A Gradual Disappearance of Insects.* 2005.
ISBN: 1-931247-22-6 $8

Kirkpatrick, Kathryn. *Beyond Reason.* 2004.
ISBN: 1-931247-09-9 $12

McCann, Janet. *Emily's Dress.* 2004.
ISBN: 1-931247-21-8 $8

Mankiewicz, Angela Consolo. *An Eye.* 2006.
ISBN: 1-931247-33-1 $9

Van Prooyen, Laura. *Inkblot and Altar.* 2006.
ISBN: 1-931247-37-4 $15

Pedraza, Venetia June. *Porcelain Dolls Break.* 2004.
ISBN: 1-931247-19-6 $7

For a complete listing of Pecan Grove Press books and chapbooks from 1987-2006, please visit our web site: *http://library.stmarytx.edu/pgpress*